Original title:

Yarrow Threads Across the Griffin Nest

Author: Lan Donne

ISBN HARDBACK: 978-1-80562-851-4

ISBN PAPERBACK: 978-1-80564-372-2

Wings of Weaving Across the Aether

In whispers of the twilight sky,
Threads of dreams begin to fly,
Stitching clouds with silver seams,
Crafting tales from woven beams.

Beneath the stars, a shimmer glows,
A tapestry where magic flows,
Wings that dance on breezy verses,
A song of flight, the heart converses.

With every knot, a story spins,
Of ancient trees and flitting fins,
Through gossamer, the flight takes shape,
A cosmic quilt, no chance to escape.

In twilight's arms, we find our grace,
Through every stitch, we leave a trace,
Of journeys walked and skies we've crossed,
In every thread, we see what's lost.

So heed the magic in the air,
For woven dreams are ever rare,
In every fiber, hope alights,
To guide the hearts through starry nights.

The Timeless Dance of Fiber and Flight

A dance of shadows, soft and light,
Where fibers twist and take to flight,
The loom's embrace, a gentle sway,
Creating worlds where spirits play.

In whispers woven, secrets spun,
A tapestry of life begun,
With every thread, a heartbeat shares,
The joy of freedom, soaring airs.

From spindle's grace, to feathered wing,
In fibers' dance, the cosmos sing,
A waltz of colors, bold and bright,
The universe, a canvas wide.

In every stitch, the past remains,
Echoes of laughter, sighs of pains,
Yet in each knot, a promise glows,
That through it all, connection grows.

So let us weave through time and space,
With every thread, we find our place,
A legacy of dreams unfurled,
In the timeless dance, we change the world.

Knots of Serenity Embroidered in Light

In corners quiet, peace abides,
Where gentle hands in silence guide,
Threads of amber, strong yet slight,
Stitched together with love and light.

Knots of comfort, woven with care,
Whispers of hope, suspended air,
Embroidered stories, rich and bright,
Each pattern tells of day and night.

Across horizons, calm and low,
Where rivers wind and wildflowers grow,
A tapestry spun from dreams of dawn,
Unraveling fears, as worries are gone.

In every twine, a breath resides,
The serenity that softly guides,
With every loop, a gentle sigh,
Of moments cherished, not saying goodbye.

So let the fibers cradle the soul,
In knots of love, we are made whole,
For in this fabric, peace we find,
Embroidered blessings, intertwined.

The Sylvan Stories of Feathered Echoes

In emerald woods where whispers play,
Feathers flutter and dance in sway,
The tales of treetops intertwine,
In echoes soft, the stars align.

Beneath the boughs where shadows sigh,
The feathered hearts in chorus fly,
Through rustling leaves, the stories weave,
Of nature's gifts, we dare believe.

With every chirp, a tale unfolds,
Of ancient myths and secrets told,
In symphony, the wild things sing,
The sylvan stories that nature brings.

As twilight drapes its velvet cloak,
In whispered notes, the forest spoke,
A gathering of spirits bright,
In feathered echoes, pure delight.

So roam the woods, let heart take flight,
For in their depths, the stars ignite,
With every flutter, let us hear,
The stories sung, forever near.

Shadows of the Guardian's Flight

In twilight's hush, they start to rise,
Guardians soar beneath dark skies.
Whispers echo in the night,
Of wings that shield from hidden fright.

With starlit eyes, they keep their watch,
In secret realms where shadows blotch.
A dance of fate in dusky air,
As dreams unfurl without a care.

Beneath the moon's soft silver glow,
They glide through worlds we cannot know.
In every heart, a tale recites,
Of shadows cast by guardian sights.

When dawn appears, their flight subsides,
Yet in our souls, their magic hides.
With courage drawn from distant stars,
They guide us through our deepest scars.

So let us trust in feathered guides,
The whispered strength that never hides.
In shadows cast by every night,
We find the power of their flight.

Tapestry of the Feathered Heart

In the loom of dreams, threads entwine,
A tapestry each heart can find.
Feathers woven through time and space,
In every stitch, a soft embrace.

Once upon a time, they flew,
O'er meadows kissed by morning dew.
With colors bright and spirits free,
They paint the world, eternally.

Through storms and calm, they hold their ground,
In gentle whispers, life's profound.
Each feather tells a story old,
Of fearless hearts and memories bold.

In every flutter, hopes abound,
A melody, a sacred sound.
So listen close to what they sing,
A love that binds through everything.

As twilight folds its arms around,
The tapestry is safe and sound.
With feathered hearts, we shall embark,
And weave our dreams into the dark.

Beyond the Horizon's Grip

A distant call from waters deep,
Where secrets blend with shadows steep.
Beyond the horizon's timid line,
Adventure blooms, untamed, divine.

With every wave that kisses shore,
A tale unfolds of ancient lore.
In sunsets painted bold and wide,
Our spirits yearn to soar and glide.

The journey calls, with every breath,
To face the whispers of the depths.
In twilight's hand, we find our strength,
As horizons stretch to endless lengths.

With courage forged in starlit quests,
We break the bounds, escape the nests.
Each heartbeat knows what lies ahead,
In fearless dreams, our paths are spread.

So let us sail on winds of fate,
With every moment, we create.
Beyond the grip of what we see,
Awaits a world where we are free.

Ties that Bind in Twilight's Glow

In twilight's grace, we gather near,
With whispered tales, we hold so dear.
Ties of the heart, they stitch us tight,
In gentle bonds that feel just right.

Through every trial, through every tear,
With laughter shared, we conquer fear.
The sun may set, but love remains,
A light in darkness, through the rains.

In moments fleeting, we find our peace,
From tangled roots, our spirits cease.
With hands outstretched, we face the night,
United strong, in hope's soft light.

For every story, old and new,
In every heart, a flame rings true.
Together, we weave life's sacred art,
In twilight's glow, we'll never part.

So let the stars bear witness still,
To every dream, and every thrill.
In ties that bind through joy and woe,
We find our path in twilight's glow.

Blossoms Beneath the Charmed Canopy

Beneath the leaves, where whispers play,
A thousand blooms in bright array,
Their colors dance, like magic spun,
In this enchanted, warming sun.

The breeze, it carries laughter sweet,
As petals drift, a soft retreat,
The gentle rustle, nature's cheer,
Inviting dreams, both far and near.

Tiny fairies, glimmering bright,
Play hide and seek in morning light,
With laughter ringing through the air,
As flowers weave a charm so rare.

Each blossom sways with secret lore,
Of ancient tales, and spirits' yore,
In every hue, a story bold,
Of magic lives, once lost, now told.

So linger, dear, in verdant glade,
Where echoes of the past won't fade,
For in this realm of soft embrace,
The heart finds hope, in time and space.

Echoing the Untamed Breeze

In meadows wide, the grass does sway,
While whispers of the wind convey,
Adventures held in breezy songs,
That beckon all where heart belongs.

The trees, they dance with ancient grace,
As shadows flicker, time's embrace,
Each sigh a story, bold yet free,
Carried forth by each wild decree.

Across the hills, the echoes roam,
In every gust, a longing home,
The secrets of the wildest wood,
A tapestry of dreams once stood.

With every breath, the spirits rise,
In harmony beneath the skies,
They weave their tales in gusts of sound,
Where echoes from the past abound.

So wander forth, and let them guide,
Through fields of wonder, side by side,
For in this dance of wild embrace,
Your heart will find its rightful place.

Spun by the Moonlit Silhouette

When twilight falls, a silver spell,
Casts shadows where the nightingales dwell,
The moon, a jewel, in the sky,
Whispers secrets that softly sigh.

Each star a witness to dreams afloat,
In the stillness, they gently dote,
On lovers who tread the glimmering paths,
Where time dissolves and magic laughs.

The world transforms beneath its gleam,
In mystic woods where phantoms dream,
Soft beams of light through branches weave,
Inviting hearts that dare believe.

And as the night deepens its hue,
The whispers tell of journeys true,
Of wishes made on shimmering streams,
In the silence that holds our dreams.

So breathe it in, this painted night,
In shadows spun by silver light,
For every magic holds its place,
And dreams take flight in soft embrace.

The Chronicle of Woodland Spirits

In twilight realms where shadows dwell,
The woodland spirits weave their spell,
Among the trees, in glades so bright,
They gather round to share the night.

With laughter ringing through the air,
They tell of treasures, rich and rare,
Of hidden paths that twist and twine,
In every tale, their hearts entwine.

Each leaf a page, each branch a line,
In stories woven with nature's shine,
Where echoes of the past resound,
And wisdom lost is newly found.

They dance in circles, joy, and glee,
With fires of ember, wild and free,
In every flicker, magic thrives,
In whispered tales, the forest lives.

So heed the call of ancient lore,
For spirits dance forevermore,
In every rustle, every sound,
The chronicle of life is found.

Woven Whispers of the Meadow

In the meadow where secrets lie,
Gentle breezes weave and sigh,
Blades of grass dance with delight,
Underneath the soft moonlight.

Colors blend in nature's song,
Where all the fleeting moments throng,
Each petal tells a story untold,
In whispers of the brave and bold.

Beneath the boughs of old oak trees,
A symphony of rustling leaves,
The earth hums with life anew,
In shades of gold and sparkling dew.

Fairies flit on silken wings,
Laughter in the melody sings,
Night blankets the vibrant land,
As dreams and wonders softly stand.

In morning's light, the magic stays,
A tapestry of vibrant rays,
Each moment crafted with great care,
In woven whispers everywhere.

Feathers in the Twilight

In twilight's hush, the feathers fall,
Like whispers down the moonlit hall,
They spiral gently through the air,
Tales of dreams with gentle flair.

Each feather holds a tale of flight,
Of wandering souls in the night,
Their journeys twist through time and space,
Each one a mark of nature's grace.

As shadows stretch, the stars ignite,
The heavens sparkle, pure and bright,
In the silence, stories weave,
Where hearts dare to hope and believe.

The owl calls from the ancient trees,
A herald of the midnight breeze,
With every beat of wings in flight,
A promise wrapped in soft moonlight.

In the embrace of night so still,
The world holds its breath at will,
For in the glow of stars above,
We find the essence of true love.

The Tapestry of Ancient Wings

In the twilight's gentle fold,
Wings of legends yet untold,
They flutter softly, dusk's embrace,
Marking time, a sacred space.

Golden threads of stories spun,
Tales of battles bravely won,
And in the shadows, soft they glide,
The echoes of the past abide.

Whispers from the ancient trees,
Rustle in the evening breeze,
Where every feather, each sweet tone,
Can sing of journeys, yet unknown.

From mountain high to valleys deep,
In dreams where time forgets to sleep,
Each moment captured, softly rings,
In the tapestry of ancient wings.

The night unveils its grand design,
A dance of fate, a life divine,
As constellations guide the way,
To realms where only dreamers stay.

Echoes of Wildflower Dreams

In fields where wildflowers bloom,
Laughter chases away the gloom,
Petals reach for the sky so clear,
In dreams of color, magic near.

Each blossom holds a fragrant wish,
Dancing through the morning mist,
The sunbeams kiss their vibrant hue,
A tapestry of life anew.

Whispers weave through stems so tall,
An invitation to one and all,
Where buzzing bees and butterflies,
Paint portraits under azure skies.

In the heart of summer's bliss,
Every moment sealed with a kiss,
Echoes of laughter, joy that gleams,
In the embrace of wildflower dreams.

As twilight falls on petals bright,
The stars awaken, sharing light,
And in their glow, we find our way,
To chase those dreams that never stray.

Patterns from the Heart of the Forest

In the depths where whispers play,
Ancient trees in shadows sway.
Leaves dance lightly in the breeze,
Crafting secrets, branches tease.

Mossy carpets, emerald sheen,
Nature's canvas, rich and keen.
Every petal tells a tale,
With every breeze, a gentle wail.

Sunbeams glimmer, fleeting gold,
Mysteries in bark enfold.
Twilight weaves a silken thread,
Upon this path, where dreams are fed.

Crisp and clear, the night descends,
Starlit skies, the forest bends.
Echoes of the wild serenade,
A heartbeat in this green parade.

Patterns pulse, entwined with fate,
In this realm, where wonders wait.
Listen close, and you might see,
The heart of the woods, wild and free.

Weaving in the Shadow of Giants

Beneath the branches, giants loom,
A world shaped by their ancient gloom.
Whispers of wisdom, old as time,
In every shadow, a tale sublime.

Knots of ivy, stories entwined,
In their embrace, the heart aligned.
Each leaf flutter tells a fact,
Of seasons changing, dreams intact.

Mighty trunks cradle the light,
Casting patterns both day and night.
Beneath their gaze, hearts gently stir,
As nature's chords begin to purr.

Cosmic dance of sun and shade,
Every moment a choice made.
With each sway, a history flows,
Between these titan's solemn toes.

Within the woods, a harmony sings,
Of roots and wings, of wild things.
Here in stillness, souls unite,
Weaving dreams in gentle light.

Whimsy and Wisdom in the Nest

High above, where sparrows play,
Nestled safely, day by day.
Feathers soft, a world perceived,
In tiny hands, love's reprieved.

Songs of joy blend with the breeze,
Rustling leaves dance with such ease.
In the nest, both small and bright,
Hope takes wing, igniting flight.

Wisdom whispers through the air,
Guiding hearts that learn to care.
In every flutter, lessons told,
In moments shared and dreams of gold.

A cradle spun from nature's thread,
Where whispered dreams are gently fed.
Every dawn, a canvas new,
Painting skies in radiant hue.

Whimsy drapes the forest floor,
In laughter's echo, spirits soar.
In this haven, joy reflects,
A cheerful song, our hearts connect.

The Soft Touch of Fluttering Dreams

As night unfurls her velvet wing,
In silence, soft lullabies sing.
A gentle hush wraps the ground,
In twilight's arms, dreams unbound.

Delicate whispers drift and swoon,
Along the path beneath the moon.
With every heartbeat, time suspends,
As shadowed realms where magic blends.

Feathers glimmer, a subtle art,
Fleeting moments steal the heart.
In echoes of a child's delight,
Dreams take flight on starlit night.

Softly glows the radiant dark,
Guiding souls with a silent spark.
In each sigh, a wish released,
A patch of peace, a sweetened feast.

Fluttering visions, a tender song,
Inviting all where they belong.
With every breath, we weave and spin,
Embracing dreams, let life begin.

Fabric of Reveries in the Blue

In the twilight, dreams take flight,
Threads of silver, soft and bright.
Woven whispers in the air,
Lullabies of hope and care.

Castles built in azure skies,
Where imagination never dies.
With every heartbeat, tales unfold,
In the fabric of dreams, we behold.

Sparkling stars like scattered seeds,
Nurturing our hidden needs.
Boundless visions, colors blend,
In reveries that never end.

The ocean hums a gentle tune,
As shadows play beneath the moon.
Through every sigh, through every glance,
We dance within this timeless chance.

And when the dawn begins to rise,
We hold the echoes in our eyes.
The fabric woven tight and true,
In the embrace of the endless blue.

The Intricate Dance of the Nesting Clouds

Suspended high, they twirl and spin,
With every gust, a new begin.
Draped in white and shades of gray,
They weave a tapestry of play.

As whispers ride the gentle breeze,
They gather close among the trees.
In secret corners, rare and bright,
Nestled dreams take off in flight.

A ballet soft, a waltz sublime,
Each puffy form, a dance through time.
They cradle secrets, old and wise,
Beneath the vast and shifting skies.

The sun peeks through, a golden beam,
Unraveling the clouds' soft dream.
A moment caught in breathless grace,
Where every heart finds its own place.

And as the twilight steals the light,
The clouds embrace the coming night.
In layers deep, their stories blend,
A symphony that never ends.

Embracing the Ephemeral

Time, like a river, flows so fast,
Moments shimmer, here and past.
In fleeting breaths, we chase the day,
Embracing dreams that will not stay.

A blossom blooms, then fades away,
With each sweet scent, our hearts can sway.
In laughter caught, in sighs that rise,
We find the light in soft goodbyes.

Each teardrop tells a story grand,
Of love and loss, a gentle hand.
Through every echo, lessons learned,
As flickering candles softly burned.

The twilight calls, a soft farewell,
Where shadows play, and wishes dwell.
In twilight moments, we reside,
Embracing all the joy and pride.

For life is rich in every glance,
In every heartbeat, every chance.
To cherish now, as time departs,
Embracing all with open hearts.

The Threads that Time Forgot

In dusty corners, secrets lie,
Threads of stories woven shy.
Whispers of those long ago,
In gentle tones, they ebb and flow.

Frayed at edges, yet so bold,
Tales of magic, love untold.
Through echoing halls, they softly tread,
Inwoven dreams where few have led.

A spider's web, a link to past,
Each fragile strand, a spell that's cast.
In shimmering lights, the stories gleam,
Threads of fate and woven dream.

To touch the fabric, old and worn,
Is to see the dawn of life reborn.
In every thread, a life anew,
Of hopes rekindled, bright and true.

And as we weave in twilight's glow,
With every stitch, our spirits grow.
The threads of time, though worn and fraught,
Will hold the tales that time forgot.

Threads of Whimsy in the Garden

In the garden where flowers bloom,
Petals dance like fairies' plume.
The sun dips low, a golden sigh,
Whispers twirl on zephyr's high.

Bees hum tunes of sweet delight,
Chasing shadows, shy of light.
Each leaf tells tales of joy and cheer,
In this realm where dreams appear.

A silver stream sings a soft tune,
While stars awaken, one by one,
Magic flutters in the air,
In every corner, wonders fair.

Footsteps lead to secrets kept,
Where gnomes and whispers softly slept.
The moonlit path, a silken thread,
Guides wanderers where dreams are wed.

With every breeze, a story stirs,
Nature's laughter, sweet as purrs.
Threads of whimsy spin and weave,
A tapestry of hearts to believe.

Between the Threads of Flight

Beneath the sky where starlight weaves,
Birds take wing, as the heart believes.
Their songs weave tales of distant lands,
Dreams unfurl with gentle hands.

When twilight wraps the world in hues,
Each feathered friend sings of the blues.
They dance on whispers, soft and low,
Carrying secrets only they know.

Clouds drift gently, a soft embrace,
While shadows play in this endless space.
Between the threads of flight, they soar,
In realms where magic opens doors.

With every dawn, their wings ignite,
Chasing the warmth, embracing bright.
Echoes of laughter fill the air,
An invitation to wander there.

So let us follow where they lead,
Between the threads, our spirits freed.
In the dance of life, we find delight,
In the song of birds, our hearts take flight.

Textures of Timelessness

In every wrinkle of the tree,
Lies a story, deep and free.
Bark intertwined like whispered vows,
Echoes of time, the earth endows.

Moss carpets soft beneath our feet,
In shades of green, a soothing treat.
Each stone cradles a memory's sigh,
Textures of time that never die.

The wind carries hints from the past,
While moments linger, held steadfast.
Faded petals, their colors bold,
Share secrets of love and stories old.

With every step, enchantments grow,
Where history's gifts forever flow.
Through branches swaying, life attests,
In nature's weave, we find our quests.

From ancient roots to skies so wide,
Textures bind us, a timeless tide.
Embrace the feel of what has been,
In every texture, let love begin.

Under the Canopy of Enchantment

Where sunlight filters through the leaves,
Magic dances, and the heart believes.
With every shadow, a story glows,
Under the canopy, the wonder grows.

Whispers fill the air with dreams,
As nature hums in glowing beams.
Crickets serenade the night,
Under the canopy, pure delight.

Mushrooms peek like hidden gems,
In the twilight's glow, they make amends.
Each fern unfurls, a gentle pause,
Under the canopy, nature's cause.

Stars twinkle in the velvet black,
Guiding us down the secret track.
With every step, the magic remains,
Under the canopy, joy sustains.

So linger here, where wonders dwell,
Under the spell of nature's swell.
For in this realm, hearts intertwine,
Under the canopy, all is divine.

Secrets Tucked in the Budding Leaves

In a realm where whispers dwell,
Secrets hid 'neath every shell.
Nature's tale in green unfolds,
Stories ancient, softly told.

Tiny buds with dreams alight,
Cradle hopes in morning's light.
Gentle breezes, tender touch,
Guard the truths we love so much.

Underneath the forest's skin,
Magic waits to breathe within.
Feel the pulse of life renew,
Hidden paths of strange adieu.

Listen close, the silence speaks,
Promises in rustling creeks.
Each leaf dances, sings a song,
Inviting all who dare belong.

In the shade where shadows play,
Secrets linger, fade away.
Yet in hearts, they find their place,
Lives entwined in nature's grace.

The Guardian's Tapestry of Stars

Above, a tapestry so grand,
Woven light by unseen hand.
Stars that flicker, twinkle, gleam,
Guardians of each whispered dream.

In the night, they softly gleam,
Guiding souls like river's stream.
Each constellation tells a tale,
Of brave journeys, love, and veil.

They shimmer in the velvet sky,
Whisper truths that never die.
Holding wishes, hopes in flight,
Their dance brings warmth to darkest night.

Gather 'round, let stories share,
Every star, a tale laid bare.
In the stillness, hear their song,
A melody where we belong.

The guardian's watch, a lighted thread,
Binding worlds where fear has fled.
In the dark, let hearts align,
With the stars, we all entwine.

Echoes of Boundless Journeys

Across the seas, adventures call,
Echoes rise where shadows fall.
Footsteps trace the land and sky,
In each pulse, the spirits fly.

The horizon beckons bold and bright,
With the promise of new light.
Every path, a tale of old,
In each voyage, memories hold.

From mountains high to valleys low,
Ancient winds of wisdom blow.
Guiding souls on quests unknown,
To find the parts they've never shown.

In whispers soft, the past we hear,
Tales of laughter, joy, and fear.
Boundless journeys, hearts entwined,
In the echoes, love we find.

As stars illuminate the way,
Every night a brand new day.
Through the stories, lost and found,
We gather peace in every sound.

Weaving Wishes in the Starlit Veil

In the night, where shadows blend,
Wishes whispered, dreams ascend.
A starlit veil, soft and bright,
Cloaks the world in tranquil light.

Threads of hope and silver beams,
Dancing softly, weaving dreams.
Every flicker, every glow,
Holds a promise, let it grow.

In this tapestry of night,
Hearts unite like stars in flight.
Each desire, a thread we spin,
In the cosmos, deep within.

Together, weaves a story vast,
An echo of the future's past.
Hold your dreams beneath the sky,
In this moment, let them fly.

With every wish, let love prevail,
In the magic of starlit veil.
Seize the night, let spirits soar,
For in these dreams, we are much more.

Feathers Entwined in Twilight

In the hush of eventide, softly they twirl,
Feathers dance lightly, in a silken swirl.
Whispers of magic, weave through the air,
Crimson and gold, secrets they share.

Under the gaze of a watchful moon,
Hearts beat as one, a sweet, silent tune.
In the twilight's embrace, souls intertwine,
A tapestry woven, fierce yet divine.

With each gentle flutter, dreams take their flight,
Curled in the shadows, engulfed by the night.
Carried by breezes that sigh with delight,
Feathers entwined, in the soft, fading light.

They gather the stars, in their tender caress,
Carving out wishes, pure and boundless finesse.
In twilight's embrace, where the world holds its breath,
Feathers of hope dance, defying all death.

Banishing darkness, like a brave, fiery spark,
Their songs paint the silence, slicing the dark.
In the glow of their flight, a promise is found,
Love ever-growing, as the night spins around.

Echoes of the Celestial Loom

In the vault of the heavens, threads shimmer and spin,
Woven by stars, where the wonders begin.
The whispers of cosmos, in symphonies rise,
Carrying tales through the vast, endless skies.

Each stitch tells a story, of battles and grace,
Of journeys untraveled, a mystical space.
In ribbons of starlight, hearts catch the gleam,
As echoes of dreams swirl into a stream.

Time flows like water, through the fingers of fate,
Intertwined destinies, love never too late.
Threads of compassion tie each soul to the next,
A quilt of existence, vibrant and vexed.

Through the loom of the heavens, we dance and we sway,

Guided by wishes that light up the gray.
Bound by the fabric of memories past,
In the echoes of starlight, our spirits are cast.

With each gentle shimmer, we find our way home,
Through realms of existence that gently we roam.
In the celestial weave, we are never alone,
For the echoes of starlight forever are known.

The Nest of Dreams and Dares

In the heart of the forest, where shadows unfold,
Lies a nest made of secrets, both tender and bold.
In the stillness of night, softly it gleams,
Cradling the hopes of the bravest of dreams.

With feathers of courage, it beckons us near,
Inviting the wanderers fueled by their fear.
A sanctuary cradled, of wishes long shared,
In the nest of dreams, no heart is unpaired.

Cocooned in belief, beneath sheltering leaves,
Whispers take flight, like the breath of the eves.
Surrounded by magic that sparks in the dark,
The nest thrives in wonder, igniting a spark.

Each branch tells a story, of those who have soared,
Unraveled their doubts, and courage they'd stored.
In the embrace of the night, their spirits awake,
The nest of dreams dances, with all it can make.

So dare to believe, let your heart be your guide,
In this magical haven, our fears set aside.
For the whispers of hope and the dares that we bear,
Reside in this nest, forever we share.

Starlit Stitches of Hope

Under the blanket of deep velvet skies,
Stitches of starlight weave through our sighs.
Each glimmer a promise, each twinkle a glance,
Inviting the dreamers to leap and to dance.

With hearts gently sewn to the fabric of night,
Hope twirls in the darkness, bathing us in light.
A tapestry shining, rich colors ablaze,
Guiding the wanderers through life's winding maze.

As shadows stalk gently, and whispers take hold,
The warmth of our wishes, in threads never cold.
Through trials and triumphs, we gather our grace,
Stitched in the cosmos, we'll find our place.

Each star sends a message, a beacon, a spark,
Illuminating paths through the depths of the dark.
With starlit creations that fly from our dreams,
Hope ever-growing, stitched into our seams.

So gather your wishes, beneath the vast dome,
With starlit stitches, we weave our own home.
For in the embrace of all that we find,
Hope whispers forever, in love deeply twined.

Mystical Weavings Under the Moon

In twilight's caress, shadows dance,
A tapestry spun from chance.
Whispers of magic, soft and light,
Under the gaze of the silvered night.

Stars twinkle like secrets kept,
In the silence where dreams have leapt.
Threads of fate tangled and bold,
Stories of mystics and heroes told.

Moonbeams stitch the fabric bright,
Weaving wonders 'neath the night.
Eyes close to visions rare,
A world unseen, a breath of air.

The fabric shimmers with ancient lore,
A portal to realms forevermore.
Each weave a story, every knot a sign,
In the quiet night, all souls align.

Veils of enchantment, woven thin,
Secrets unfurling, where dreams begin.
A tapestry rich with life's embrace,
Under the moon, time finds its place.

Needlework of the Enchanted Sky

Stitching stars to the fabric of night,
Galaxies swirling, a wondrous sight.
With every prick of the needle's point,
The cosmos hums, a celestial joint.

Clouds drift softly, whispers of light,
Sewing the horizon with threads of white.
Each stitch a promise, a wish on the breeze,
Carried forth by the rustling trees.

Moonlit patterns, each thread unique,
Voices of the ancients, softly speak.
In the tapestry of the wide expanse,
The heavens unfold in a timeless dance.

Needles of starlight, twisting and turning,
Ignite the dark with magical burning.
Each constellation, a story unspun,
In the needlework of skies, life's begun.

The night is a loom, the world an art,
Knots of fate binding each heart.
Beneath this tapestry, we dream and sigh,
In the needlework of the enchanted sky.

Threads of Silk amid Hidden Realms

In the heart of the forest, where secrets flow,
Threads of silk in the moonlight glow.
Whispers of faeries in delicate threads,
Binding the dreams in the places we tread.

Hidden realms dance in shadowy light,
Weaving the tales of the falcon in flight.
Every silk strand a portal anew,
To lands where the wildflowers bloom and grew.

From spider's embrace, the magic unspools,
Looming through echoes of mystical rules.
Each flicker of light, a prickle of spine,
Entwined in the magic, the realm is divine.

In twilight's embrace, the threads intertwine,
Guarding the secrets where mysteries shine.
Woven together in harmony's grace,
The silk of the night knows every face.

With each whispered breeze, magic weaves tight,
Holding the dreams in the soft silver light.
The threads of silk draw us close, yet far,
To hidden realms where the wonders are.

Guardians of the Spiraling Threads

Deep in the forest, where shadows merge,
Guardians stand at the magic's verge.
Spiraling threads that shimmer and twine,
Weaving the fates where the stars align.

With hands softly raised, they cradle the night,
Guardians weaving destiny's light.
Each thread a heartbeat, a life's gentle sway,
In the dance of the cosmos, they guide the way.

Ribbons of starlight, glowing so bright,
The guardians sing to the moon's silver light.
In chambers of time, they watch and they weave,
Crafting the stories, the hopes we believe.

Every knot holds a tale untold,
Secrets of ages, both fragile and bold.
The spirals spin softly, winding us in,
A tapestry woven, where life can begin.

With each gentle pull, a heart finds its song,
In the fabric of life, we all belong.
Guardians of threads, we honor your guise,
For in your embrace, our dreams shall rise.

The Woven Secrets of the Night

In twilight's clutch, the shadows creep,
Whispers of secrets, the stars keep.
Moonlight dances on leaves so bright,
Weaving dreams through the fabric of night.

A tapestry spun with silken threads,
Of magic and wonder where time treads.
Each twinkle a tale, a story to tell,
In the hush of the dark, where echoes dwell.

Through ancient trees, the breeze softly sighs,
Carrying knowledge of the wise.
The night unfurls its mysterious scroll,
Revealing the depths of every soul.

As lanterns of fireflies flicker and glow,
Guiding lost hearts through paths below.
In the woven secrets, the truth lies near,
Waiting to be sought without any fear.

With a flutter of wings, the darkness breaks,
Awakening dreams as the dawn awakes.
For in the night, where the magic reigns,
Lies the beauty of life, in its subtle gains.

Fantasies in the Hollow of Eternity

In the hollowed realms where whispers reign,
Fantasies bloom like forgotten pain.
Time intertwines in a dance so grand,
Holding close the dreams of a faraway land.

Each heartbeat echoes in endless flow,
Carrying tales of what we don't know.
In the depths of silence, secrets unfold,
Woven in starlight, shimmering gold.

Upon the canvas where shadows play,
Fading like dusk into the day.
Every breath a promise, every sigh a wish,
In the fabric of time, we are free to exist.

Glimmers of laughter, snatches of song,
In this hollow of dreams where we all belong.
Each moment a thread, each thought a hue,
Painting the vastness in shades anew.

As eternity calls with its gentle allure,
Our spirits embark on paths so pure.
In the tales we weave with our hearts entwined,
Live the fantasies of a world unconfined.

When Dreams Soar on Gossamer Wings

When dreams take flight on gossamer wings,
The air fills with hope as the nightingale sings.
Through the veil of sleep, they gracefully glide,
Carried by wishes like waves of the tide.

With every dawn, they whisper and wane,
Fleeting as shadows, yet vivid as rain.
In the softest embrace of the starry skies,
Echoes of laughter, the heart's sweetest sighs.

The sky's a canvas where colors blend,
Stories unravel, and dreams never end.
A tapestry woven from the fabric of light,
Illuminating paths through the velvet night.

So flutter along on those delicate beams,
Chasing the visions that dance in our dreams.
For life's fleeting moments are fragile and bright,
When dreams take to flight, we soar with delight.

In the quiet of night where our visions reside,
The magic of dreaming becomes our guide.
With wings of a whisper, we embrace the serene,
As hope carries us forth on the wings of a dream.

A Glimpse into the Nesting Light

In the cradle of twilight, the stars softly gleam,
Holding the secrets of a world in a dream.
Whispers of warmth in a tender embrace,
A glimpse into magic, the nest of our place.

The flicker of fireflies, like wishes alive,
Illuminates paths where our hearts can thrive.
Each sparkle a beacon, a guide in the night,
Leading us gently into the light.

Here in the stillness, the heart finds its song,
Where we weave together and finally belong.
The nesting light wraps us in its glow,
Fostering dreams that silently flow.

Among the shadows, the fabric entwines,
With tales of the past that the present defines.
In this embrace, we find solace and peace,
As the nesting light whispers, let worries cease.

A glimpse of enchantment, of life intertwined,
In the winged silence where love is defined.
Forever we wander, forever we roam,
In the glow of the night, we find our true home.

Nestled in Nature's Embrace

In a glen where soft winds sway,
Whispers dance through leaves at play.
Sunlight weaves a golden thread,
Cradling dreams where spirits tread.

Mossy carpets, emerald deep,
Awaken secrets ancient keep.
Boughs bend low, with grace they bend,
Nature's wonders never end.

Crisp air filled with fragrant pine,
A gentle stream, a silver line.
Here in stillness, hearts can rest,
Nature's arms, forever blessed.

Songs of birds, a lilting sound,
Echoes soft, around, around.
Every breeze tells tales untold,
Nature's mysteries unfold.

Nestled deep in nature's care,
Every moment, pure and rare.
In this haven, life takes flight,
Wrapped in warmth, by day and night.

Secrets of the Sylvan Grove

Beneath a canopy of dreams,
Where sunlight spills in golden streams.
Murmurs rise from roots below,
Tales of time in soft winds blow.

Whispers flutter, shadows play,
Hidden paths, a magic way.
Every branch a story spins,
Every leaf a secret wins.

Violet blooms and ferns so green,
In this realm, magic is seen.
Twining vines and colors bright,
Guide the wanderers in flight.

A tapestry of life unfolds,
In this grove, the heart beholds.
Each flutter, each rustle, a chance,
To sway along with nature's dance.

In twilight's glow, the stars align,
Kindred spirits, spirits divine.
In this grove, dusk softly calls,
As night descends, enchantment falls.

The Twine of Time's Embrace

Moments weave like threads of gold,
Time entwines, both warm and cold.
In each heartbeat, echoes blend,
Stories woven, paths extend.

Dappled shadows, time's own art,
Marking journeys, each a part.
Memories dance on winds of fate,
Binding lives, both small and great.

Through the tapestry of dawn,
Life unfolds, a fragile yawn.
In the twilight, soft and slow,
Time reveals what we may know.

Threads of laughter, threads of tears,
Knit together through the years.
In the loom of fate, we find,
Woven hearts, forever blind.

Embrace each twine, each gentle seam,
For in this weave, we dare to dream.
Life's adventure, winding, vast,
Time embraced, as shadows cast.

Beneath the Watchful Sky

Underneath the vast expanse,
Clouds drift by in a lazy dance.
The sun and moon, a steadfast pair,
Guard our dreams, with utmost care.

Stars whisper in the velvet night,
Guiding souls with silver light.
Each twinkle, a promise, a sign,
That in the dark, we still can shine.

As dawn awakens the sleeping brook,
Nature's canvas, paint and book.
Color spills from sky to sea,
A masterpiece of purity.

Beneath this dome where wishes soar,
Hearts entwined, forevermore.
In every breeze, a tale to write,
Beneath the watchful sky, so bright.

With every sunset, shadows play,
As dusk bids farewell to day.
In this realm of endless skies,
Magic lingers, never dies.

Labor of Love in Feathery Silks

In twilight's glow, a loom does gleam,
Threads of silver, a weaver's dream.
With every stitch, a tale unspools,
A dance of passion, love that fools.

The feathery touch of heartstrings tight,
In the hush of dusk, they spark the night.
Each delicate weave, a bond so rare,
Crafted with joy, imbued with care.

Colors collide in vibrant embrace,
Shades of longing, time cannot erase.
A tapestry bright, where hopes entwine,
In the fabric of love, their hearts align.

As dawn approaches, the work shines bright,
Every thread whispers a promise of light.
In feathery silks, the labor of hearts,
A masterpiece born, where love never parts.

The Guardian's Embrace Amidst Threads

In shadows deep, a guardian stands,
Woven in warmth, with gentle hands.
Amidst the threads, they weave their care,
Each pull and tuck, a silent prayer.

With every stitch, a smile is spun,
The heart of a child, each battle won.
A cloak of safety, protective and tight,
Threads of love forged in the night.

In the guardian's embrace, worries cease,
A haven crafted, a quilt of peace.
With edges frayed or patterns wild,
Each woven piece tells of a child.

Through laughter and tears, the fabric grows,
Binding the souls, where affection flows.
Amidst the threads, a sanctuary lies,
Woven with dreams and loving ties.

The Dance of Nature's Quill

With nature's breath, the quill takes flight,
In ink of dusk, it writes the night.
Petals swirl in a fragrant breeze,
A dance of quills through whispering trees.

Each stroke a melody, soft and sweet,
Capturing moments, where heartbeats meet.
In the pages of time, the dance unfolds,
Stories of life in verses bold.

Twinkling stars in the inkwell's sea,
Each spark a wish, wild and free.
The quill pirouettes 'neath a silver moon,
Crafting enchantment, a timeless tune.

With nature's path, the quill reveals,
The beauty of life and its many seals.
In every line, the essence we trace,
In the dance of nature, we find our place.

Nestling Hopes in the Woven Dream

In the cradle of night, where shadows sigh,
Hopes take flight, like stars on high.
Nestled in dreams, softly they play,
Woven whispers guiding the way.

Through branches woven with silken threads,
The promise of dawn in the nest where it spreads.
In twilight's hold, aspirations gleam,
Each moment cherished, a heart's pure dream.

Under the moon, the dreams converge,
Life's winding path, where wishes emerge.
With every breath, new stories unfold,
Nestling hopes, where love's warmth is told.

In the tapestry formed by a gentle hand,
Each woven hope a soft, brave stand.
For in the nest of a loving heart,
Dreams take root, never to part.

Whimsy of Fabled Aviaries

In castles high with feathery grace,
Where larks weave dreams in a sunlit space,
A chorus of colors fills the morning air,
Whispers of magic, everywhere.

With wings of gold and hearts so free,
They dance on breezes, wild and carefree,
Each note a story, each flap a rhyme,
Carried through tales of olden time.

Beneath the boughs where secrets sleep,
The sparrows sing and shadows creep,
A tapestry woven in the glade,
Where fables of beauty will never fade.

Through swirling mists and emerald light,
They twirl through dusk and into night,
Each feather a brushstroke, bold and bright,
Painting the dreams that take flight.

In every chirp, a wonder's call,
In fabled aviaries, we find it all,
A world where whimsy ever gleams,
Alive in the magic of our dreams.

Pathways Through Untrodden Realms

Beneath the moon's enchanting glow,
Pathways weave where few dare go,
Each step a whisper of fate unseen,
In tangled woods where shadows lean.

Through brambles thick with tales untold,
Adventures shimmer in hues of gold,
A flicker of light, a rustle of leaves,
The heart of the forest quietly believes.

Footprints lead through the misty vale,
Where fairies flit and dreamers sail,
Beyond the realms of mundane sight,
They gather stories in the night.

The stars above, a guiding map,
In silence deep, where the brave may nap,
Each corner turned reveals a friend,
In pathways where the wild winds bend.

So venture forth with eyes anew,
To untrodden realms where magic grew,
For in the heart, a wanderer lies,
Through pathways spun 'neath painted skies.

The Legacy of Fluttering Shadows

In twilight's hush, where secrets sigh,
Fluttering shadows gently fly,
Tales of yore on whispered wings,
Echoes of time as stardust sings.

A dance of phantoms, soft and light,
They weave through dreams in the velvet night,
Chasing the glow of fading stars,
Bearing the weight of ancient scars.

As night unfolds its velvet cloak,
With every flutter, a new tale spoke,
In gardens where the wild things roam,
The shadows return to guide us home.

Their legacy, a timeless blend,
Of laughter, sorrow, and love to mend,
Each flutter speaks of worlds unseen,
In whispered tones, they intervene.

So listen close when shadows dance,
For in their song, you find your chance,
To soar with dreams, and never part,
Embrace the legacy of the heart.

Whispers of the Weaving Winds

In softest breath, the winds do weave,
A tapestry of stories to believe,
Through valleys deep and mountains high,
A gentle hum beneath the sky.

With every gust, a tale unfolds,
Of distant lands and legends bold,
Nature's chorus sings in tune,
Under the watch of silvered moon.

They dance through glens where silence thrives,
In whispers, the wind awakes our lives,
Each murmur carries a hope anew,
In winding paths, the old and true.

As seasons change and time takes flight,
The winds remain, our hearts ignite,
For in their song, a promise lies,
To chase the dreams beneath the skies.

So let the whispers guide your way,
In weaving winds, find peace and sway,
For every breeze that sweeps and spins,
Carries the truth of where love begins.

The Sapphire and the Shimmering Thread

Beneath a sky of velvet blue,
A sapphire glows with ancient hue.
It whispers tales of time and fate,
Of dreams entwined, of love's estate.

A shimmering thread, so finely spun,
Guides the hearts of everyone.
It weaves through night, it binds the day,
A bond that never fades away.

In twilight's grasp, the colors blend,
A tapestry where sorrows mend.
With every stitch, a memory caught,
In the heart's canvas, all is wrought.

The sapphire's light, a beacon bright,
Illuminates the edges of night.
In its glow, the shadows dance,
Inviting souls to take a chance.

A tale of magic, old yet new,
Where hope and courage dare to strew.
Each thread a story yet untold,
In the weave of time, both brave and bold.

Crafting Whispers of the Wind

In the hush of dawn, the breezes play,
Crafting whispers that softly sway.
Each gust a word, each sigh a song,
As nature crafts where we belong.

The leaves, they dance in sun's warm light,
Sharing secrets from day to night.
The flowers nod, their fragrance sweet,
As every heartbeat feels complete.

Through fields of green, the stories flow,
Of summer dreams and winter's snow.
The wind, a bard, it roams so free,
Unveiling all that's meant to be.

In every rustle, joy takes flight,
A promise born within the light.
As whispers linger, hearts ignite,
In the tapestry of day and night.

So listen close, let silence guide,
For whispers hide where dreams abide.
Each breeze a note in life's grand score,
A symphony forevermore.

Twilight's Fabric of Reverie

When twilight drapes the world in gold,
A fabric rich with stories told.
The stars emerge, a shimmering lace,
Weaving dreams in their warm embrace.

The moonlight spills on whispered streams,
Gilding the night with silver beams.
Each shadow grows, a secret blight,
In twilight's arms, we find our light.

With every breath, the dusk unfolds,
A tapestry of threads and folds.
In twilight's glow, our spirits soar,
As visions dance on a mystic shore.

In reverie's heart, we find our way,
Through the veil of night into the day.
Each moment wraps like fabric spun,
In twilight's weave, we become one.

So linger long, in twilight's time,
Let dreams take flight, let souls align.
For in this space, our hearts entwine,
In the fabric where the stars align.

Shimmering Silks in the Heart of Night

In the heart of night, where shadows dwell,
Silks shimmer softly, casting a spell.
Threads of silver, woven in dreams,
Embracing the dark in glimmering beams.

The stars adorn this velvet sea,
Embroidering tales of what could be.
With every flicker, a story ignites,
In the silken cloak of starry nights.

Whispers of secrets, echoing low,
In the tapestry where moonbeams flow.
A dance of shadows, a waltz so sweet,
In shimmering silks, we find our feet.

Each stitch a heartbeat, each knot a vow,
To cherish the moment, to live for now.
In the quietude, where dreams take flight,
We wear the silks of the heart of night.

So close your eyes, let magic weave,
In shimmering darkness, let us believe.
For in this space, where dreams unite,
We find our magic, the heart of night.

Textures of Dreaming Night

In shadows deep, where secrets play,
The moonlight weaves its silver ray.
Soft whispers drift on velvet air,
Through tangled dreams, both light and rare.

Stars above, like scattered seeds,
Garden of hopes where imagination feeds.
A tapestry spun from quiet sighs,
In every glance, a new surprise.

Misty paths of twilight's gleam,
Where every heart embarks on a dream.
With flecks of gold and strands of blue,
The night reveals what's known and new.

Echoes carry on gentle tides,
From where adventure and wonder resides.
In the weave of night, we seamlessly drift,
Each thread a tale, a precious gift.

So let the night cradle your soul,
In textures of joy, you will be whole.
For in each whisper, a world takes flight,
In the grand embrace of the dreaming night.

The Guardian's Gentle Fabric

Beneath the cloak of evening star,
The guardian watches from afar.
With gentle hands, they craft the day,
Into a fabric, serene and fey.

Threads of gold and lavender lace,
Woven with care, a warm embrace.
Every stitch holds a tale untold,
Of courage fierce and hearts of gold.

With whispers soft like a lullaby,
They weave through dreams that never die.
In twilight's fold, fears fade away,
A guardian's love, forever sway.

So close your eyes and feel the fold,
Of stories waiting to be behold.
In layers rich, find peace and light,
An endless wrap in tranquil night.

As dawn approaches, you shall find,
The guardian's fabric, kind and blind.
In every dawn, a new day's grace,
A gentle touch, a warm embrace.

The Trail of Whispering Wings

In meadows where the wild blooms sway,
A symphony of whispered play.
With wings that flutter, soft and light,
The tales of day give way to night.

Each whisper carries joyful tunes,
The echoes dance beneath the moons.
Through skies where dreams and hopes take flight,
I've followed the trails of pure delight.

Butterflies, like scattered dreams,
Weaving through soft, silken beams.
In their flight, a secret flows,
Of endless stories no one knows.

Listen close, the nightingale sings,
Of adventures wrapped in feathered wings.
Each flit and dart, a playful tease,
In twilight's arms, the heart finds ease.

So chase these trails, and let them lead,
To whispered wonders, hearts that heed.
For in the flight of each small thing,
Lie hidden worlds the shadows bring.

Lullabies of Silk and Stargaze

Beneath the blanket of endless skies,
Dreams unfurl like soft lullabies.
In starlit threads, the night unfolds,
Eternal tales of love retold.

On silken winds, through cosmic streams,
We drift along in tender dreams.
Each twinkling light, a guiding star,
Whispers of hope from near and far.

The moon's embrace, a silver sigh,
Cradles each wish as time slips by.
In gentle pinions, the heart finds peace,
With quiet moments, sweet release.

So hush now, close your weary eyes,
And let the stillness fill the skies.
With lullabies that softly play,
A soothing balm for the day's dismay.

In dreams, we dance on clouds so free,
Entwined in silk, eternally.
For every heart that dares to dream,
Shall find their joy in moonlit beams.

Guardians of the Hearth

In the glow of ember light,
Shadows dance like restless sprites,
Whispered tales from days of yore,
Guardians watch, forevermore.

Around the hearth, the warmth does swell,
Stories weave a magic spell,
With every crack, and every sigh,
Dreams take flight and with them, fly.

Spirits rise from ashes deep,
For those we love, their promises keep,
Rising smoke and gentle breeze,
Tell of hopes and memories.

Through darkened woods and silent nights,
These faithful ones, with guiding lights,
Wrap us in their gentle care,
In every heartbeat, they are there.

Until the dawn breaks through the mist,
We hold on tight to all we're kissed,
For every hearth will ever stay,
A sacred bond that will not fray.

Serpentines of the Woodland Realm

In the green where echoes rise,
Serpentine paths twist 'neath the skies,
Wonders dwell in whispered hues,
Secrets held in morning dew.

Mossy stones and ancient trees,
Bending softly to the breeze,
Nimble creatures dart and play,
Guardians of the woodland way.

Hush now, hear the tales they weave,
In each shadow, something to believe,
Moonlit nights and starlit paths,
Guide us with their subtle laughs.

Beneath the boughs, the magic breathes,
Rustling leaves as wisdom seethes,
In every fork, a choice to make,
Embrace the fate that we partake.

And when the twilight calls us forth,
To wander realms of hidden worth,
We rise, entwined in nature's dream,
In serpentines, we find our gleam.

Threads of Light at Dusk

Threads of gold and dusky gray,
Knit the sky at end of day,
Whispers flutter on the breeze,
As daylight dips behind the trees.

Each fading ray, a tale retold,
Of sunlit paths and hearts of gold,
As stars emerge, the night unfolds,
In silver blankets, dreams behold.

Quiet moments steeped in time,
Life's sweet rhythm, soft as rhyme,
Dancing shadows, fleeting light,
Chessboard patterns of the night.

In twilight's arms, we pause to ponder,
Every thread a wish to wander,
Through untold realms, where moments blend,
At dusk, the magic has no end.

So linger here 'neath evening's glow,
Let the gentle currents flow,
For in the silence, we may find,
The heart's true echo, intertwined.

The Call of the Celestial Guardian

In the quiet of the night,
A whisper calls, a guiding light,
Through starry vaults, the echoes sing,
For fear not, child, of what may spring.

Celestial beings, soaring high,
With wings of light, they roam the sky,
In stardust dreams, they weave and thread,
Protecting all who dare to tread.

Each twinkle bears a wish so true,
The universe listens, waits for you,
In every heart, their grace does bloom,
Chasing away the shadows of gloom.

So take a breath, feel their embrace,
In sacred silence, find your place,
For in the vast celestial sea,
Lies the call to who you're meant to be.

Trust the journey that unfolds,
Celestial guardians, tales untold,
With every star, your spirit soars,
As love and light forever pours.

The Spellbound Weaver's Narrative

In the heart of the twilight glow,
A tapestry waits, woven slow.
Threads of magic, whispers of fate,
Each stitch a secret, dreams await.

Beneath the loom, the shadows dance,
In the fabric's weave, a mythic trance.
Fairy tales spun in colors bright,
Weaver's fingers trace the night.

With silver and gold, the patterns twine,
Stories entwined, both yours and mine.
In every corner, legends twine,
Bound by the stars that brightly shine.

The loom hums gently, a lullaby,
As hours weave into the sky.
Each knot a place where worlds collide,
In this sanctuary, all dreams abide.

When dawn breaks forth, the colors burst,
Casting spells, quenching our thirst.
In this realm where tales regenerate,
The Spellbound Weaver holds our fate.

Harmony in the Nesting Realms

In the cradle of leaves, a soft tune flows,
Where the magic of nature quietly grows.
Birdsongs flutter through the warm air,
A symphony woven beyond compare.

Nestled in branches, the secrets lie,
Whispers of wonder, a soft lullaby.
From twig to feather, the promise sings,
Of love that blossoms and the joy it brings.

The murmur of streams in bowls of stone,
Echoes of laughter, a world to own.
In harmony's arms, we find our place,
Among the wonders of nature's grace.

Where sunbeams dance on a silver thread,
And dreams take flight, unbridled, widespread.
In the nesting realms where origins start,
Love, like a nest, cradles every heart.

So let us wander in nature's embrace,
Finding our rhythm, our destined space.
In unity's flight, our spirits soar,
In the nesting realms, forevermore.

Celestial Echoes in the Threads of Time

In the vault of night, the stars convene,
Whispers of ages, eternally seen.
Threads of silver, weaving the past,
Echoes of moments, forever to last.

With each twinkle, a story unfolds,
Of lovers and legends, of hearts bold.
Through shadow and light, the cosmos calls,
In the tapestry drawn on infinity's walls.

Galaxies spin in delicate dance,
In the waltz of the heavens, a cosmic romance.
The fabric of time, both fragile and grand,
Woven by voices that once took a stand.

As moons wax and wane, destinies shift,
In the celestial quilt, we find the gift.
Each heartbeat echoes in the silence vast,
In the threads of time, our essence is cast.

So gaze at the stars, let your spirit climb,
Embrace the echoes in each rhythm of time.
For within the cosmos, we all align,
In the celestial weave, our fates intertwine.

Patterns Adrift in the Cosmic Sea

In the depths of the night, a cosmos unfurls,
Stars like whispers in the look of swirls.
Patterns adrift on the velvet tide,
Where dreams take flight, and mysteries hide.

Waves of stardust, they beckon and sway,
Painting the heavens in brilliant display.
With each gentle pulse, the galaxies spin,
Under the watch of the moon's silken grin.

The heart of the universe beats in time,
To the symphony sung by the celestial chime.
In this cosmic sea, the essence flows,
With currents of fate where the starlight glows.

Each constellation, a story retold,
The ancients protect it, steadfast and bold.
As we navigate through wonder's abyss,
In patterns adrift, we find our bliss.

So let us sail on this astral sea,
Embracing the patterns that set us free.
For within each wave, a chance to see,
The connection that binds you and me.

Dreamscapes Laced with Wonder

In twilight's glow, dreams softly weave,
A tapestry of magic, hearts believe.
Whispers of starlight dance through the air,
Each wish a promise, unspoken, rare.

The moonlight bathes the world in grace,
A realm where shadows spin and chase.
Through velvet skies, our hopes take flight,
In dreamscapes laced with pure delight.

The trees hum secrets, old and wise,
Each leaf a story beneath the skies.
A symphony of colors, vibrant and bright,
Painting the canvas of endless night.

Laughter echoes in the sylvan glade,
Where time stands still, and dreams are made.
In this enchanted world, we roam free,
With wonder as our guide, eternally.

As dawn approaches, the dreams must fade,
Yet in our hearts, their magic stayed.
For every dream that touched the ground,
A spark of wonder still can be found.

The Harmony of Flight and Fabric

Wings of gossamer brush the skies,
In a dance of freedom, where the spirit flies.
Threads of light entwine in the breeze,
Weaving moments that the heart believes.

Each feathered dream takes a daring leap,
An artistry crafted, both bold and deep.
In the fabric of air, a story's spun,
Where the song of the wind has just begun.

Across the heavens, tales intertwine,
With each beat of wings, a spark divine.
Fabrics woven from courage and grace,
Crafting a journey, time can't erase.

Like clouds that drift in a balmy sea,
Floating along in sweet harmony.
The whisper of flight speaks to the soul,
An endless pursuit that makes us whole.

In every ascent, there's magic anew,
The sky, a canvas, painted in blue.
With wings and fabric, our spirits unite,
In the harmony of flight, pure and bright.

Of Wings and Looms

On ancient looms, where dreams are spun,
Wings of wonder beckon, calling us on.
Each thread a memory, vibrant and bold,
Stories of flight in patterns unfold.

The weaver's hands, with delicate grace,
Crafting the whispers of time and space.
Each stitch a heartbeat in the tapestry wide,
Binding the heavens with earth side by side.

From the depths of the sky, the fabric descends,
In spirals of color, where magic transcends.
With wings as the needle, the loom starts to hum,
We dance with the winds as the moments succumb.

The flight of our dreams unfolds with delight,
Under the gaze of the moon, oh so bright.
In a tapestry woven with laughter and tears,
The song of our souls resounds through the years.

Of wings and looms, the legends are spun,
In every creation, a journey begun.
As threads of our lives interlace and twine,
We find our own stories, forever enshrined.

Celestial Weavings in Nature's Embrace

In nature's embrace, the cosmos flows,
Stardust and petals in soft repose.
Each flower blooms with the light of the stars,
A symphony woven from Venus to Mars.

The forest whispers, secrets concealed,
Celestial patterns in quiet revealed.
From earth to sky, where galaxies meet,
Each heartbeat echoes a rhythm so sweet.

Among the branches, the constellations sway,
Telling stories of night blending into day.
With every rustle, a tale takes form,
In the cradle of wonder, safe from the storm.

Thus, the heavens weave their gentle art,
In every rustling leaf, a tale to impart.
Celestial weavings, where magic adheres,
In nature's embrace, we lose all fears.

So let us wander where spirits reside,
In the realms of enchantment, side by side.
For in this tapestry of life and grace,
We find our home in the universe's trace.

Embers of Enchanted Layering

In the heart of a forest, secrets dwell,
Where whispers weave like a magical spell.
The light through the leaves paints a tale,
Of dreams that shimmer and soft winds that sail.

Amidst the shadows, fairies play,
With laughter that dances like sun on the gray.
Each flicker of fire, a heart ignites,
In the wonder of night, where enchantment invites.

Old stones whisper of stories gone by,
While starlit sky hums a lullaby.
Through veils of mist, ancient souls roam,
Guardians of magic, they call this home.

The embers glow bright in the dark of the night,
Guiding lost wanderers, lending them light.
In forests enchanted, where spirits abide,
A tapestry woven, in nature they confide.

Here, amidst the roots, truth intertwines,
With the pulse of the earth, the magic aligns.
In every heartbeat, in every sigh,
The embers of life are the dreams that we try.

Flight of the Ethereal Protector

Above the canopy, a shadow glides,
An ethereal guardian, where mystery hides.
With wings like whispers, it soars through the sky,
A watchful protector, ever so nigh.

Through valleys and peaks, its presence is felt,
In the rustle of leaves, where the earth's pulse is dealt.
It shields the lost with a gaze warm and bright,
Bringing hope to the weary who wander the night.

In dreams it descends, a figure of grace,
With solace as soft as a comforting embrace.
In twilight's embrace, its song calls the brave,
To rise like the dawn, to stand, not to cave.

The stars weave a pattern, a map to unfold,
Of journeys uncharted, of tales yet untold.
Across the celestial fabric, it sweeps with delight,
A guide for the wanderers, a flame in the night.

With each breath of the wind, a promise is made,
That the flight of the protector will never fade.
Through realms of wonder, through shadows and light,
The ethereal guardian takes flight in the night.

Harmonies of the Verdant Refuge

In the midst of emerald leaves so fine,
A refuge glimmers, a realm divine.
Where rivers hum in melodic streams,
And every flower dances with dreams.

Beneath the wide expanse of azure skies,
Whispers of nature in harmony rise.
Birds in the branches compose their own songs,
A symphony vibrant where each note belongs.

The earth cradles life in its gentle embrace,
Fostering beauty in every place.
With roots that entwine like lovers' hands,
The verdant refuge forever stands.

In glades of soft sunlight, shadows play,
From dusk until dawn, night steals the day.
The harmony lingers in breezes so sweet,
Inviting the weary to pause, to complete.

As twilight descends, stars shimmer in dance,
Echoing stories in a mystical trance.
In the heartbeat of nature, the truth is revealed,
In harmonies sung, life is forever healed.

The Fabric of Celestial Echoes

Woven in starlight, threads intertwine,
A tapestry formed through space and through time.
Each glimmer a story, a journey unknown,
In the whispers of cosmos, the seeds are sown.

From the depths of the void, where silence prevails,
Echoes of worlds drift through luminous trails.
Galaxies dance in an infinite sway,
In the fabric of night, they beckon and play.

Cradled in moonbeams, dreams take their flight,
As shadows and light collide in the night.
The universe sings in a voice deep and clear,
A melody carried, for all hearts to hear.

In realms uncharted, where wishes take form,
The cosmos unfolds, like a mythic storm.
Every heartbeat resonates, every breath a spark,
In the fabric of time, creation embarks.

So listen to nightfall, embrace the unknown,
For the echoes of starlight have wisdom been shown.
Through tapestry woven, at destiny's call,
In the grandeur of cosmos, we're part of it all.

Woven Wonders Beneath the Moonlight

In silver glow where shadows dance,
We find a world of secret chance.
The whispers of the night unfold,
As dreams are spun from threads of gold.

A tapestry of stars appears,
To weave together hopes and fears.
Each glimmer tells a tale anew,
Of magic cast in midnight dew.

The moon, a lantern in the sky,
Guides wandering souls as they fly.
Each stitch, a bond of heart and mind,
In shadows deep, our dreams entwined.

So let us roam through night's embrace,
Where nature weaves a mystic space.
For in this realm of gentle light,
We find our path through velvet night.

With every breath, the magic stirs,
In moonlit glades, where wonder whirs.
Embrace the night, let worries wane,
In threaded dreams, we'll dance again.

Threads of Timeless Whimsy

With playful threads of shimmering hue,
We stitch our laughter, bright and true.
In every twist, a story sings,
Of curious hearts and fanciful things.

The fabric of our days is spun,
With joy and whimsy, never done.
A patchwork quilt of memories bright,
Warming souls through day and night.

Each thread a moment, small yet grand,
Woven with care by gentle hands.
In patterns bold, or soft and sweet,
Life's joyful dance, a rhythmic beat.

Through realms of whimsy, laughter roams,
In every stitch, we find our homes.
Embrace the tales that laughter weaves,
For in the heart, the magic cleaves.

With every fray, new dreams take flight,
In threads of joy, our spirits light.
Let's weave our wishes, soft and bright,
In fabric's fold, a pure delight.

The Beauty in Tangles and Twists

In tangled yarn, a beauty lies,
Like whispered secrets, soft and sly.
Each knot a tale of love and pain,
In winding paths, our hearts remain.

The twists and turns, a dance we share,
Through life's design, we learn to care.
For in the chaos, moments gleam,
A tapestry of hopes and dreams.

We find our strength in knotted threads,
As laughter mingles with our dreads.
In every loop, a lesson learned,
In every twist, our passion burned.

Embrace the mess, let spirits rise,
For beauty blooms in tangled eyes.
In each entanglement, love persists,
A cherished gift, as fate insists.

So dance amid the knots of life,
Through trials faced and moments rife.
In tangled strands, the magic lingers,
A wondrous tale that time still fingers.

A Nest of Infinite Possibilities

In cozy nooks where dreams take flight,
A nest is built with soft delight.
With whispers shared and laughter bright,
Possibilities bloom, a wondrous sight.

Feathers gathered from skies above,
Each stitch a story, told with love.
In every corner, magic thrives,
In cradled dreams, our passion dives.

The warmth of hope, a gentle thread,
In every heartbeat, tales are spread.
From tiny seeds, our futures grow,
In boundless nests, the joy will flow.

A tapestry of heart and kin,
In unity, our quests begin.
Through every thread, our spirits soar,
For in each nest, we seek for more.

So gather 'round, let dreams ignite,
In cozy nests, we share the light.
With open hearts, we craft our place,
In infinite realms, we find our grace.

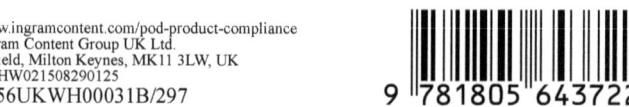